THE SUMMERHOUSE POEMS

a second collection of poems

by Dorothy Pope

The Summerhouse Poems
First published in 2008

Published by Dorothy Pope
10, Runnelfield, Harrow on the Hill, Middx. HA1 3NY

ISBN 978-0-9542719-1-6

Printed and bound by CPI Antony Rowe,
Eastbourne

In Memory of Michael

Contents

Famous

A starlit, lamplit balcony of stone
and you and I some yards apart – your son,
my husband, off somewhere – and you, alone
in shadowed alcove drinking wine – what fun
it would have been to talk to you, I thought.
I had real things to say, a few in fact,
not just fan's gush. I longed to speak. You caught
me looking at you twice, was glad of tact,
enjoyed your solitary drink but when
the bell for Hamlet's final act recalled
us all and people bottlenecked back in,
you joined me, strolled me in as my reward.
"Bit parky," you remarked, and to this day,
your charm's what I remember, not the play.

Old Clothes

The L-shaped alleyway afforded shade,
a triangle of makeshift privacy,
and here two tramps of indeterminate age
sealed a transaction of such charity

that day in March of bitter wind. One owned
just trousers and a pair of laceless shoes,
no more, and these he wore of course. His friend
was richer by two shirts and one of these,

the one not on his back, he held aloft
as though for Sir's approval, gave away
his surplus. And the first man took the gift
for warmth and more respectability.

He put it on in wordless gratitude —
this in the shadow of a grand hotel.
What I there witnessed makes me feel subdued
when I remember it, which I do well.

Lombardy Poplar

Secluding, landmark, cherished tree,
we had to bring your great self down.
Your lower reaches were diseased
despite you lovely leafy crown.
Your upper eighty feet of health
were pedestalled on rot. I groaned
but if I had not had you felled
you would have fallen on your own.

Skilled men arrived here at first light,
efficient, practised team of six.
One climbed your swaying, plumose heights.
Five stood below to pick up twigs
and foliage, then logs. Your twin
trunks outlined now against the sky
though dignified stood, starkly thin,
uttering a silent, plaintive cry.

Methodically you were reduced.
Still lower down, where you were wide
your heavy wood had to be sliced
quite thinly. Oh! Where now your pride?
Mourning, I paid my last respects
to your still grand, eye level stump.
A few more necessary cuts
then six brooms briskly swept you up.

Losing His Looks

Not my usual dentist –
the filling-in one ha ha –
but my usual crumbling off
of huge white berg of tooth
from jagged molar cliff asunder
so there I was.

Not looking up, he drawled my name,
bored lips an inch from rim
of coffee mug reluctantly put down,
left radio racket on and door ajar,
mumbled, "Right lower six or seven,"
resented question, put temporary patch,
said, "You can go,"
while looking somewhere else
and drank the other half
without goodbye.

Well, your loss, mister.
Dehumanising me diminished you
and will do every time you treat
a human being like a thing.

You trade on your good looks,
been doing so for years
but let me tell you something else –
you're losing them, those looks,
replacing them with what you are.

I'll have your patch replaced quite soon
by my proper dentist. She knows how
to treat both teeth and people,
polite, engaged, professional,
her sweet face pretty with humanity.

The Misses Sharpe

They gave up trying to teach and quell
unruly pupils, leased this shop
and now, with strict regard to health,
serve lunches. Mind you, not a drop
of fat is used and portions are not large,
light lunches what they say and what they mean.
You go out feeling righteous not indulged,
your diet still intact, your stomach lean.
Stern notices are everywhere.
"One chef with just one pair of hands
can only do so much.", "We serve
in strict rotation please note." and
"It's hot food after twelve – our rule."
Eat up or stay in after school?

Country Church

So unexpectedly, the first we saw
in this eight hundred year old house of prayer
on opening the great and well oiled door
were several dozen jars of jam ranged there
atop a table labelled with which fruit,
suggested price, if jam or jelly, proof
of someone's love of God, all capped with cute,
pinked hats of gingham, "to preserve the roof".
The church – huge, spare;
   light streamed through good stained glass,
four hundred pews, mere twenty hymn books out
but new embroidered kneelers, gleaming brass,
fresh flowers within, grass being mown without.
No actual sermon preaching trust and love;
these and the jam were eloquence enough.

Family Home, Lincolnshire

and from the summerhouse, the view
is, first, that unmarked area of grass,
where stood the Air Force quarters of a few
of England's Few, that rings with silent laughs,
our chipping green for practice golf. Beyond –
the orchard's gorgeous blossom, later fruit
for village children and the Anderson,
now apple store. Then, topiary in privet
and in box; my sculptor's hands can see
the shape inside the mass. By Perkins' grave,
a clump of perfect daffodils blow free
of London's politicking stress. I have
a cherished weekend refuge where I come,
say, "Hello, House. Restore me." I am home.

written for a friend

Evening

Through my window, I can see
a woman, Titian-haired and young.
She's reading, on the bench beside her,
half a dozen large white daisies
picked at forest's edge from thousands
casually graceful as her
dainty ankles, sandalled feet.

Quite unaware of her great beauty,
she reads on from book, whose paper
jacket, upside down, deceives
a strolling airman into thinking
she's pretending. So emboldened,
he approaches, sits beside her,
blue eyes never leaving hers,
which, in turn, marvel at his charm and
handsome blondness, tall, hard slimness.

After some sweet conversation,
exploratory, tentative,
they rise and saunter off together
through the trees towards the village.

and I know, yes, know they do.
They marry, make a home and baby –
parting six years on for ever.

As the vision of them fades,
the cocoa trolley rattling round,
I wonder wistfully just where
he went those sixty years ago.

Housewife

With busy needle, thimble, treadle,
she turned bed sheets sides to middle,
let down hems, inserted lengtheners.
Pockets made patch elbow strengtheners.

Every inch of her back garden
grew successions of abundant
vegetables, fruit – delicious,
picked to eat with same-day freshness.

Plums preserved in lines of bottles,
jam in jars and onions pickled,
serried rows on shelves in pantry
testament to her. No entry

in a book ever recorded
how she worked. Quite unrewarded,
just the striving for perfection
gave her all her motivation.

Surely there's nobility,
a true, though quiet celebrity,
when such a woman daily tries
with little means to reach the skies.

1916–2000

Was there a summing up, a reckoning?
And if so, was there happiness enough
on balance then to die with sweet relief?
Or did you rail that life had failed to bring
you thrill, fulfilment, cherished blessings, things
that you looked back on with delight – the stuff
of living? Bleak indeed if weeping snuffed
your brave but flickering flame, with wanting's stinging
tears. Better that you were by then too ill
to think regret for I suspect you would
have felt a disappointment far too sad
to contemplate. God grant you had one pillow
picture you could focus on, one good
contenting ending in that narrow bed.

January

The drab sky wears a uniform of greys.
Below, in ridged and stone hard, frozen ground
no scarlet petticoats of petals found
that flirt their frills from hems of summer days'
green skirts. Now, naked hedgerow's thorned embrace
elbows the robin as he shouts his bounds.
In chilling winds, torn rags of tattered clouds
are dragged, dull streamers, through the wintry skies.
The stoic oak withstands the piercing cold,
moss stockinged trunk, enduring branches bare.
The thin fox trims his pride and eats from plate
of put out bread and scraps, no longer bold,
in humble gratitude accepting fare.
The earth and all its kind hold fast and wait.

The Joys of February

St Valentine's Day; snowdrops game salutes;
a grateful robin, coexisting fox,
both scrounging hopefuls in their fluffed out suits;
the glow from stepping out to letterbox
in cleansing cold, returning from the post
to welcome warmth, the cosiness of home
with wheeled in trolley bearing buttered toast,
and curtains drawn against the teatime gloam;
the still, quiet mornings with a landscape white
with thinning mist or trace of frost on grass,
a watered sun diffusing kindly light.
Mad March will bluster and all this will pass.
Till then – the lovely last of wintertime.
I think this underrated month sublime.

April

An English spring appears
and, quintessential and afresh,
the primrose peeps,
its orange eye a-sparkle
with held raindrop,
pale yellow velvet petals
nestled like a clutch of eggs
within the wrinkled folds
of quilted moist green leaves –
consistent miracle of sixty
well-remembered springtimes.

Mid August Looking To September

The early morning garden is a thrill
of cool before the August day's begun
to burn and undermine the energy and will

to work or even move. The noonday sun
will scorch and reach the eighties Fahrenheit
but in a fortnight summer will be done.

Its busy hemispheric round will be complete.
The sun, though merciless, must then confess
to failing, moving on, its powers deplete,

no longer able to depress and stress
so that I sweat and fret with silent groan,
relinquishing its licence to oppress.

September and I'll come into my own!
September sees the tyrant overthrown!

Cool Morning

Mid August, even so, a faint hint, gift
of autumn momentarily – a sweet,
soft breeze. With slender branches trees entreat
a sift of foliage. Their fingers lift.
Then half a dozen paper leaves adrift
blow in and dance round summer sandalled feet,
though brief, their restlessness another fleeting
sign of imminent and massive shift.
The season's on the very cusp. We'll see
the great sun climb and midday will be hot
but morning now, as evening later, spares
relentless sultriness, humidity
with temperate caress. Long shadowed autumn's
in the wings. The old earth cools, prepares.

September

With what relief I greet your temperate
self, September, breathing
energising cool, diffusing quiet
light that's merciful on skin
that flinches, eyes that shrink
from ruthless August grill and glare -
no more lethargic, sweaty sitting
out of time, just getting through
but living. Waking up refreshed
in airy room, quickening with
a working health I feared I'd lost,
I'll pick up projects, mop up backlog,
move around with swiftness, vigour
as the season turns – September.

In My View

Resurgent daisies stud the summer grass
and from the peanut basket bluetits swing.
Abundant in their numbers, never sparse,
resurgent daisies stud the summer grass.
To me these winged and petalled gems surpass
the stinted beauty of the diamond ring.
Resurgent daisies stud the summer grass
and from the peanut basket bluetits swing.

Another of Your Wordless Gifts

Playfully you place
in different arrangements every day,
the three lace cushions on our bed.

Though two are bigger than the third
and of a different design,
all are crocheted, cotton, square and white

and I would not have thought
so many permutations possible
as those that you think up for me.

As well as all potential orderings
of A and B and C, of course – that's six –
I'm finding diamonds and squares,

lines with spaces and without,
straight and sloping rows and columns,
dipping in the middle or with one otherwise displaced.

Parallel, symmetrical or not
I think they'll be repeated soon
but no they're all and always different.

Your intellect, capacity for play,
are inexhaustible as is the love
which likes to find a daily way

of saying, wordless writing
on the great, white wedding cake-like bed,
"This, should you chance to notice, is for you."

My Best Poems

are not written
on neat sheets of paper
or on the backs of envelopes at public tables.

I beam them at your picture hooks
and dance them down your garden paths.
I breathe them in the folds of your white shirts,
smile them into your grey eyes
and laugh them on our talking walks,
your jokes fresh as bread.

Your Squarer Hands

How many dozen cupboards, hundred shelves,
what desks and tables, paths and steps,
sheds, hutches, sandpit, ponds and toys,
accoutrements for all our homes,
you've made for our convenience
and joy: unspoken compliments,
your gifts, the broken mended straight,
designs and wishes realised.
Hands age. Unshod, they leather up,
each thickened finger history.
I watch your hands about your book,
their slimness gone, a testament
to sacrifice to generous love –
now even dearer, squarer hands.

Refectory Table

Daydream a while and see
its salvaged, oaken mightiness
peopled.
Along its length on benches,
little boys intently watch
the head-of-table prefect
charged with carving
into eighteen equal shares
not just the raisin-ed pudding
but the syrup soaked
deliciousness on top.
Apportioning a basin shape
takes skill as well as fairness.
Look harder.
See one little boy,
small fry with grey-blue eyes.
Identify your father.
See him again, a prefect now,
scrupulously fair and capable.
Bless him,
my day-school sons,
and hold this table dear.

Breakfast

Laid at bedtime, neat and ready,
his inviting breakfast table –
though her husband's still in bed he
loves to know that when he's able
to descend the stairs he'll find it
waiting for him. There his Times and
bright brass teapot stand behind it,
wall clock with its ticks and chimes and
marmalade with toast and butter,
plate and dish, his mug clean gleaming –
all that's needed but no clutter.
She delivers porridge steaming
then retires, leaves him with kisses.
This is what domestic bliss is.

Hard Frost

A night frost following an early spring
has blighted the magnolia. Now browned,
its petals droop and fall, a littering
like yesterday's confetti on the ground.

Where is its glory now, perfection's blush
that stopped me as I walked to gaze and gaze?
That just one silent stroke could do so much
by stealth to spoil its subsequential days!

The man who walks his dog said, "Never mind.
There's always next year to look forward to,"
but what, of course, he could not understand
was that to me the lovely tree was you.

You, darling, cannot bloom in future years.
Your petals a finality – my tears.

The More Condemned

Who bear the greater loss, those who die first
or those condemned to living on alone?
Who suffers more, the tender or the nursed
since lovers feel each other's pain as own?
Your deprivation is of further life,
mine, loss of you, which is the living death.
Is widowhood, that travesty of wife,
more painful than the stopping of the breath?
Pray all the gods that I could take your place
and spare you all the suffering ahead!
Your pain would be less hard for me to face
and you could carry on when I was dead.
Conjecture's idle. Part of this bad news
is that we are not privileged to choose.

Orange Blossom

A shower of philadelphus petals spill
onto your slippered feet and silvered hair
as you, my dying bridegroom, come to fill
the peanut feeder for the birds. And there
among cascading flowers, your thinness stretched
up to a branch, with waiting bluetits near,
you're silhouetted, memorably etched,
and then your white shirt seems to disappear
in snowy camouflage. Soft breezes sift
a silent, sprinkled gift of blossoms here.
Though I interpret every perfumed drift
as golden wedding tribute, also clear
is that this dense confetti is your shroud.
Behind unquiet eyes, I cry aloud.

To Michael

You are more dear to me than meat or drink.
The rapture and the tenderness you gave
in fifty years that passed by in a wink!

I worried but I did not really think
that you would go before me to the grave
for you're more dear to me than meat or drink.

Life was a joy when you were in the pink
of health. We rode upon a crested wave.
Now fifty years will pass by in a wink

because your healthy armour had a chink
in which a cancer grew to break, enslave
you, who are more to me than meat or drink

and all my love can't make your tumour shrink
nor you endure no matter that you're brave,
and fifty years will pass by in a wink.

Oh darling, we are on the very brink!
A minute more is what I've come to crave
for you're more dear to me than meat or drink
and fifty years have passed by in a wink.

Men of Peace

How sweet and fitting. This I thought as I
shook out the cloth of wisps of hair your kind
and gentle hairdresser had left behind.
This being spring, prospecting birds will spy
these silver snippings eagerly and fly
them off as trove, an unexpected find.
Not strong enough to feed them now, you've lined
their nests. Your garden is regarded by
all territorial birds as neutral ground,
a feeding station. Here they've called a truce and found
a sanctuary. Your father died. He fought
for peace at Ypres and Passchendaele. He thought,
agreed, that "dulce et decorum est......."
and you, you've fed the birds and lined their nests.

Teacher's Love

I wrote a semicolon upside down!
I read it later on in disbelief.
Grammarian if nothing else, I frown.

I know what caused my punctuator's crown
to slip. Your illness, concentration's thief,
is why my semicolon's upside down.

I see you writhe beneath the eiderdown.
Disease invades what should be sleep's relief.
Grammarian, I sorrowfully frown

to think that "Michael", favourite proper noun,
could be brought low. In adoration's grief
I wrote a semicolon upside down!

I rail in unavailing vigil's gown,
"But fifty years is mere aperitif!"
Grammarian, I watch and grimly frown

to think my lovely man perhaps might drown
in pain and be no longer *substantif*.
I wrote a semicolon upside down!
Grammarian, if nothing else, I frown.

June Drop

And as I sat, a well formed apple fell.
It lay there looking perfect, beautiful.
Why this one should have failed I could not tell,
its June drop seeming inexplicable.
Compared with those left on the tree to thrive
and those already down, it seemed to me
a certain candidate, sure to survive:
unblemished, firm, well fastened to the tree
I would have thought, its stalk robust to see,
an icon apple, healthy, fine and green
but now, by scarcely noticed tragedy,
reduced to what it was and might have been.
A few days and its glory will be spent.
No reason then. A random accident.

Golden Wedding

His anniversary gift, exquisite thing
she gazes at and gratefully admires,
adorns her finger, turquoise opal ring
of old antiquity and quiet fires.
They celebrate their fiftieth year today
though only forty-nine years married. They're
anticipating by twelve months the day
he will no longer be alive to share.
The opal tokens sorrow and October –
the end and the beginning of their love:
the Hallowe'en ball where they met each other,
the days remaining being not enough.
This opal, then, a twofold message sends
of rapture and of heartbreak as it ends.

Bird Sanctuary, August 2004

Salt marshes and we're watching birds.
The birds oblige, abound. My son and husband
show me avocets and bearded tits,
waders wading, shovellers shovelling,
greylag geese in sudden flight,
largely silent, sometimes crying

and largely silent, sometimes crying,
I am watching my two men.
Always heart-meltingly alike,
their differences now impress:
strong, tree trunk legs, the wasted thinness,
full rosy face, pale, sunken cheeks,
the muscled neck, the slender stalk,
the striding, the mere keeping up.

The picnic lunch, the snapshots taken –
last photographs, last holiday.

A Different Game

It's Scrabble our late Sunday evening game
but soon it's clear that something is amiss.
She's focused but her playing's not the same.
A four for SAD? She's never played like this.
Unconsciously, she's choosing words not score
we realise, and every tile she lays
in PAIN and SUFFER is one dry tear more.
Another wasted S in LOSS. She plays
out, and in one sense never playing better,
her grief. I test my theory with RAVE
and, sure enough, she uses her blank letter
as a G and turns it into GRAVE
with downwards GONE. And then the still unshed.
She's lost the game and weeps a dry-eyed DEAD.

Shadowed

On Christmas Eve the unimagined news –
a shadow on the not quite routine scan
so tiny it was hard to comprehend
that it could have significance – bemused
then, as it sank in, stunned us. He would lose
first health then life. Inoperable cancer
ruthlessly decreed my lovely man
would die of its insidious intrusion.
One last passion banquet in our bed,
we salvaged joy from wreckage from then on.
Slow minutes raced: a holiday, the things
that had to be endured, prepared and said.
The six months stretched to more but then were gone.
Long shadowed autumn waited in the wings.

Bare Boards

No respite for in sleep there are the dreams.
Last night I was required to play the bride
in a school play – request, as sometimes seems,
obligatory, not to be denied.
I went along. The women dressing children kept
on, busily absorbed in known routine,
and when I asked where I could find the script
they scarcely paused to shrug. No men were seen.
I searched the school for needed script but found
no-one who knew, perceived the need, recalled
there ever being a director round
or bridegroom or supporting cast. Appalled,
unscripted, unrehearsed, I realised
that on that awful stage one improvised.

Not Yet

Unread and daily set aside
to be recycled,
his copy of The Times arrives
and I
can no more bear
to cancel it
than I can part
with his good overcoat
or give away
his favourite marmalade.

Puffer Train

Exhaling smoke and belching steam,
huge iron engine eating fire,
remembered, loved G.W.R.
in livery of brown and cream,

your so impatient, snorting cough,
the random, serial slams, the "Mind
the doors!" your couplings' clank and grind,
guard's flag and whistle and the off.

Past each suburban garden shed,
and washing line, the staring child
that waved, to cows in patchwork fields,
now in the proper countryside.

You settled into rhythmic thrum.
We leaned back with contented smiles
of clocking up the easy miles
in synchrony – der der der dum

Then tunnel cut through sandstone rock
with windows closed against the soot's
pervasiveness, the specks and smuts,
out to the beauty, thrill and shock

of sparkling, turquoise Dawlish bay.
With cuffs and collars black with grime
and hair that reeked of smoke, on time,
the journey part of holiday.

Daisy Chain

On such an afternoon as this, I sat
in summer grass and made a daisy chain,
my first, aged four, all eagerness, once taught,
to link the little flowers. I see again
that meadow somewhere deep in Warwickshire,
my mother with her dreamy hazel eyes,
contented, sitting separate but near,
I concentrating on my enterprise.
And when she judged it long enough, she did
the tricky job of joining end to end,
then placed it, coronet, upon my head
and with her Brownie box preserved me, crowned.
Unbidden, half forgotten, these thoughts rise
of mother, daisies, learning, childhood skies.

The Shawl

I would not part with it for all the world,
potato-shaped, red, white and royal blue,
brave flag of your dear infant love unfurled
in all its ugliness upon my new
bought crib. What could a foster mother do
but hug and thank your loving self aged six,
prescribed by doctors for our barren state?
Sweet medicine, you had worked and, thanks to you,
I had conceived. The news produced no mix
of feelings, jealousy not in your nature.
Welcoming him, you laid joyful plans
and crocheted oddments, this despite the keen,
sore wretchedness of eczema on your hands.
Unloved, unwanted as you'd previously been,
I wonder you knew how to love at all.
Proof that you did – this lovely, ugly shawl.

Evacuee

She washed up in a shoreside terraced cottage
fostered by a Devon couple, gentle,
loving, in this haven came to know
the heaven of a sandy beach. With pail
and wooden spade, she reconstructed house,
cathedral, school and sweetshop under skies
with no more in them than unworried gulls
which skimmed her pet name here of Dimples, limned
in capitals, in sand the perfect stage
of damp, with edge of spade and then with shells.
She paddled in the playful waves with squeals
of new delight, quite cleansed of dread. In bed,
tucked, lulled, she breathed, in sleeping synchrony,
the soothing music of the rhythmic sea.

Misunderstanding

On Christmas morning nineteen thirty-eight,
I woke to extra magic. I'd believed
their talk of Santa, tree and presents but
no one had mentioned snow. On Christmas Eve
the world had been its usual brown and green.
This morning every outside inch was white.
Knee deep, this stuff, my first, and only seen
in books. The crisp of it! The cold, the wet,
the everywhere of it, to touch, to marvel,
tramp your boots a track of six inch prints
and see the coal and dustbins beautiful.
I registered this rare coincidence
as guaranteed, expected it next year.
Though Christmas came, the snow failed to appear.

Lupins, Radishes and Oak Tree

Before the fall, the twin great falls,
I had a garden one yard square,
prepared and sowed it, tended it
attentively. With minute care
and solemnly, I watered it,
twice daily scanned for signs my seeds
had "germinated" (fine new word!),
waged war on brash, invading weeds.

September nineteen thirty-nine
sowed first unease and then neglect.
Another new word: "Germany" –
I listened, watched, came to detect
what adults thought to keep from me.
I'd anyway learnt how to read.
My radishes grew woody, long,
my lupins browned and went to seed.

Momentously, I started school.
Of greater moment came The Blitz.
I realised a house could fall,
how marriage could be fragile, its
sereneness be a thin facade,
a brittle thing that cracked and broke.
These days I have a garden. Though
its lupins, radishes invoke

my childhood one, the difference is
a marriage solid as its oak.

Homecoming

For years I've dreamed of coming home
to Cornwall, place where I was born.
Now here, I am both overcome
and quite at peace. Those things foresworn
to live in cities, beautiful and wild,
delight and slot back into place
to that self I was as a child.
I know this sand, wind on my face,
the turquoise and the pewter moods
of this west country sea, to me
the only sea. Red earth alludes
to patchwork fields of memory.
Dear God, what fate caused me to stray?
Now here, how can I go away?

No Picnic

Ironically, they rode a tandem bike,
that warring pair, though any two less like

to live in tandem would be hard to find.
He rode in front. She took the seat behind.

They quarrelled as they puffed up Devon hills.
"You pedalling?" "Of course!" "I swear it feels

as if you're not," he snarled. He spoke his mind.
She held her tongue sometimes thinking it kind

and wiser since the sidecar held their child,
a two year old aware and watchful of their wild,

abuse. Inevitably came the rift.
The front, the back, the sidecar came adrift.

He took their money, bought himself a car
and left. The woman panicked, married far

from suitably – again – sank without trace.
The infant washed up in a Home for Waifs.

Casualties

By night the bombs rained down from dreadful skies;
by day his blows assailed her frightened eyes.
By night it was allowed to utter cries;
by day she stifled them for otherwise

their infant and the neighbours would have guessed
and so she hid her bruises, unconfessed.
She knew his rages mainly stemmed from stress,
from weeks of nightly fear and sleeplessness

but he had lost control, continued wild
long after enemies were reconciled.
Now brutalised, he would not be beguiled
and left her penniless to rear their child.

In Your Shoes

In your shoes, I'd have wondered what I'm like,
as woman now, and how I was at school.
Did you not ever ask yourself, awake
at night perhaps, if I was beautiful
or clever, happy, mother now to boys
who looked like you, as handsome, tall and blond,
or if, for want of funds and fathering, all joys
had come to nothing, not survived beyond
the day you left us, broke? Life was deprived,
of course, but you gave me a legacy
I prize. You left me hypersensitised
to cruelty and worth – rare gift. I see
right through facades. Not spared a second thought,
I'm fine — though I'm the daughter you forgot.

Suffer Little Children

My vividest school image is Miss Black's
sadistic face. She taught with relished smacks.
You learnt your spellings out of dreadful fear.
And in December on the wall each year
the same three stencilled camels caravanned
across a paper frieze of yellow sand,
her token tribute to His birth. By Christ!
You learnt your tables or next day got twice
as many hardest slaps on naked thighs
as you had made mistakes. The faces, cries
of those who could not learn! She'd stoop to thrash
to get a better purchase on defenceless flesh.

Then, after years of misery in Miss Black's class,
a miracle for children came to pass.
Stacked tables slipped and fell on Miss Black's head
and she summarily joined the unmourned dead.

Vanishing Cream
a spell to make a teacher disappear

Hocus pocus, stalk of crocus,
eye of moke that's out of focus,
tongue of lizard, hair of wizard
minced up with a turkey's gizzard –

stir the brew and let it stew.
Cook it through till it turns blue.
Round it dance till in a trance
then advance with ghastly chants.

Paste it thinly on our books
so that when she comes and looks
she'll inhale the noxious fume
disappearing from the room.

Jimmy Spink's Comeuppance

The great and handsome silverback
knew no English, felt no lack.
It understood the class clown's chants
were insults as he rudely pranced

and wagged a finger at arm's length
and mocked and jeered with all his strength,
"You are ugly!" twice because
he sought his sycophants' applause.

Unnoticed, the intelligent beast
lowered its long arm the least
bit, scooped a handful of its poo
(very wet that day) and threw

it through the cage bars hard, you've guessed,
at Jimmy's unsuspecting chest.
The cronies howled in deep disgust,
made off, declaring Jimmy must

spend the school trip day alone,
its being more than flesh and bone
could bear, that nauseating stink,
and so, a chastened Jimmy Spink

was far from popular, was spurned,
and lonely, sorrowfully, learned,
in solitude and circumspect,
the lesson: Must show due respect.

How Dumb Can You Get?

Humpty Dumpty sat on a wall.
Humpty Dumpty had a great fall.
Well, I ask, what did he expect?
Eggs have no right sitting erect
with no cup or nest for support.
Having no flat base you'd have thought
he'd have utilised better sense,
known a wall (or gate or a fence)
is no place for parking, an oeuf
being one continuous curve.
And, of course, he's brittle as hell
clad in that impractical shell.
Rather save your sympathy for me
Rockabye-ing Baby in a tree.

Holiday

The family's away.
Hooray! We can play!
Each spider and flea
Feels suddenly free
And becomes acrobatic.
Mice swing from the attic.
Importunate beds
Laugh and stand on their heads.
Yelling pans will beat time,
Slamming doors, clocks that chime
Adding rhythm. In pairs
Waltz Chippendale chairs,
Abandoned, unchecked.

Yet **they** never suspect.

More Nonsense

"They went to sea in a Sieve they did"
against their friends advice.
"You'll capsize, sink and drown. You'll see."
But they sailed optimistically.
They took a dozen balloons to buoy
them up and paper hats for joy
and safety pins, profiteroles,
and chewing gum to stop the holes.
They told dry jokes when they got wet
and played a tenor clarinet
to blow the Sieve sides dry.
They visited exotic isles
and greeted people there with smiles
and all in all it was so nice
they got back home with hearts aglow
and friends said, "There, we told you so."

Nostalgiad

Oh for a taste of Fuller's Walnut Cake!
Good as she is, my mother cannot bake
one that's a patch. I positively ache
to cut a slice and delicately take
a fingernail sized portion, just a flake
of that incomparable icing, make
its fragile eggshell crispness slowly break
down on my tongue, and blissfully partake –
translucent white, a tad short of opaque,
a work of genius and no mistake.
Though there are copies more than you could shake
a stick at, I can recognise a fake
at forty paces so, for pity's sake,
have mercy. Bring back Fuller's Walnut Cake!

Ink In The Veins

I view computers with a Luddite scorn.
This generation doesn't know it's born.
The thrill of writing words down never fails me.
It is a cure-all for what ever ails me.
A few sheets of blank paper and a pen
to start the day with and I'm fit again
to face the hazards of the world. Don't think
to transfuse me with blood. Just give me ink
in an emergency; it pulls me through.
Black's best but at a pinch then blue will do.
My fountain pen connects to hand and brain,
fits in my bag, can be used on a train.
It snugly feels just like a part of me
and ink flows from the very heart of me.

Day Off

Time at last to get something done!
I'll reckon my income tax return,
weed out old clothes, put shoes in pairs
and clear my desk and clean the brass,
hem the torn curtain, wage righteous wars
on accusing cobwebs and bursting drawers,
organise myself at last,
tick every job off this long list.
I may even tackle and tidy the shed.

Turns out that I, late from my bed,
lingered thinking, in my bath,
slumber's dreamy aftermath.
Breakfasted, I read the paper,
solved the crossword and, much later,
finally deciding what to wear,
wandered out and, pausing there,
admired the beauty of a rose,
appreciating with my nose,
watched birds, and velvet bees at flowers.
I dined, read poetry for hours,
traced double rainbow through the rain
and went back to my book again,
had long conversation with a friend
as though the day would never end
then, yawning, stretching like a cat,
realised it was bedtime. So that was that.

Life Begins at Eighty

Yes, life begins at eighty. It is true.
You get excused all kinds of nasty chores
like washing dishes. As for gardening you
just say you're far too frail, must stay indoors.

You do feel up to telly, food and games,
describing how life was between the wars.
Pretending to be deaf or daft are claims
which never fail to silence crashing bores.

Come lunch-time, you can leg it to the table
then aver that indigestion gives you pause.
A large postprandial brandy gets you stable
before the most uninhibited of snores.

At half past three, you rouse for tea. You've found
that exercise is best kept to the jaws.
At eighty you're so proud to be around,
you think you're due a big round of applause.

Seal

Approaching from the unfenced side
we walked along the sands to see the seals
among their pups the day our mother died
and, at one of the nursery creeks, my heels
dangling in the stream, I stroked the soft,
new fur of one of month-old twins. It arched
its baby head and met my eyes. It coughed
a baby bark while nearby mother watched
in stationed vigilance. The day before
the funeral we visited again
but this time, mother seal was oft somewhere;
her pups were independent, had outgrown
their need of her. And so it was with us
I realised. Our mother knew that truly
we were strongly grown now and, at peace,
had slipped away. And we felt peaceful too.

written for a friend

I Wonder

The road of excess leads to the palace of wisdom.
Proverbs of Hell. William Blake 1757 – 1827

True happiness and wisdom lie
where two divergent roads rejoin.
They both arrive there by and by
but very different ways traverse.
The one is self denial's route,
excess, the other course.

Denial's stony and austere.
You know the constant agony
of deprivation and desire
as strained as if on rack and wheel
and only after years emerge
proof against what you feel.

Excess, though bringing downfall's shame,
knows heady pleasure's running cup.
Perhaps the climb back to good name
is worth the bold experiment
that pleasures body, heart and mind –
repletion's deep content.

I chose denial's way and, in
arrival's safety, dare look back
down both the roads and wonder if
I should have spared myself the pain
by opting for the other choice
and known the joy of sin.

Those Feet

(with apologies to William Blake)

And did those feet, a lovely thought,
tread England's grasses sandal-shod
or is this mere idea, caught
in wishful thinking's web? He's trod

the walkways of the mind of man
world-wide for centuries and so
to want Him here in Avalon
is natural but can we know?

The facts add up and there are years
of His life unaccounted for.
A thorn tree for His crown of tears
is rooted on this English shore.

The rational remain aloof.
"It's possible," our minds admit,
"though only that for lack of proof."
Yet instinct clamours, "I know it."

In Praise of Slow

Daydreamers know they only seem
to spin the world who rush and steam-
roller the money making scheme
with workaholic self esteem.

In hammock hung from apple bough
ideas come, it's not known how.
Inventors, poets all avow
the idling mind's the one endowed

with thought. The Newtons, Wordsworths know
the fruitfulness of going slow,
of gazing, musing, strolling so
let's pause awhile and wiser grow.

From a Chair by the Window

Thanks be that I am gifted with a garden
that's deciduous, alive with growth
and change, not stiff with static evergreens
but seasonally varying. These trees
each day present afresh as tenements
for busy birds, as quick with leaf and hue,
and underfoot, from snow to crocus,
petalled earth to acorns, leaves then snow again.
This moving and maturing scene unfolds
the years, though imperceptibly, as sure
and certainly as aging ticks the tiny
seconds till a million minutes mount
up incrementally and finally
I find they've moved the present to the past.

Hiatus

The threading pattern of the china beads
along the necklace friends have brought me back
from China is disrupted and this leads
me to imagine why, and who lost track.

Instead of long and round alternately,
at one point, I've two round beads wrongly placed
together and I fancy I can see
how this arose. Two girls, best friends, sweet faced,

work side by side at threading beads by hand.
Sometimes, they liven the monotony
by whispering a confidence behind
their hands like schoolgirls at illicit glee,

then work, still giggling spasmodically,
and having lost the rhythm they had had.
Their heads-together break has given me
a necklace with a flaw. And I am glad.

Famous (p 7) won second prize in a Literary Review competition

Old Clothes (p 8) won first prize in an Oldie competition

The Misses Sharpe (p 11) was published in Equinox

Country Church (p 12) won first prize in and Oldie competition

Family Home, Lincolnshire (p 13) was published in The Spectator

Housewife (p 15) was published in The Lady

Cool Morning (p 15) was published in The Spectator

Orange Blossom (p 21) was commended in a Torbay competition

Men of Peace (p 33) was published in an anthology

Teacher's Love (p 34) won second prize in an SWWJ competition

Golden Wedding (p 36) won first prize in a Winter Witch Books competition

Bird Sanctuary, August 2004 (p 37) won third prize in an SWWJ competition

Bare Boards (p 40) was published in The New Writer

The Shawl (p 44) was a runner up in a St Petroc's competition

Lupins, Radishes and Oak Tree (p 47) was published in The Lady

No Picnic (p 49) was published in The Spectator

In Your Shoes (p 51) won the Poetry Society's Hamish Canham Prize 2007

Vanishing Crème (p 53) was a runner up in a Spectator competition

Holiday (p 56) was a runner up in a Spectator competition

More Nonsense (p 57) was commended in a Spectator competition

In Praise of Slow (p 65) was a runner up in a Spectator competition

From a Chair by the Window (p 66) was published in Poems in the Waiting Room